AN INTRODUCTION TO T.M.

An Introduction to TM

by

MAIR FENN

THE MERCIER PRESS
DUBLIN and CORK

The Mercier Press Limited
4 Bridge Street, Cork
25 Lower Abbey Street, Dublin 1

© Mair Fenn 1978

Reprinted 1979.
Reprinted 1985.

ISBN 0 85342 539 6

Printed by LITHO PRESS CO., MIDLETON.

Contents

Foreword

The Transcendental Meditation programme has within ten years become a major branch of science. At the same time it has opened up a flowering of life for over two million people as it is a sublimely simple method for restoring vitality and developing latent abilities fully. The growth of this knowledge has been so unprecedented and vast that it has brought its own special needs, one of which is for simple, clear and above all personal accounts such as the one Mair Fenn has given us.

The full range of scientific research on the Transcendental Meditation programme is now so sophisticated that it is a speciality in its own right. It is certainly beyond the grasp of a quick review, even by the most advanced physiologists and physicians. This is one reason why the scientific world has not reached a consensus; there are actually very few scientists whose training (and vision) has proved to be broad enough to encompass the range of knowledge necessary—extending from quantum physics, through biology, medicine, psychology and social sciences.

Interestingly enough, it has been physicists, rather than medical doctors, who have shown us the full significance of the newly rediscovered but ancient levels of expanded awareness that Maharishi has unfolded for all people to enjoy. Some of the greatest minds in physics today are recognising that human consciousness is much more than it has been taken for, and may actually represent the deepest level of nature, the wellspring of all the forces of creativity and patterning that direct the entire flow of evolution. As this reality is coming to light it is being more often realised that the humblest people—you and I—have at their disposal all the creative intelligence of nature by means of which anything—and I mean anything—can be accomplished at will.

To me the delightful thing about Mair Fenn's book is the way she shows us how obviously, yet quietly, our own consciousness works its power of infinite correlation in everyday life. Nature hears our thoughts. She gives us what we think about. It is as if on the surface we all live in separate little rooms, while deep within we all join hands with each other and with nature in a beautifully co-or-dinated, world-wide experience of bringing about the Age of Enlightenment on earth. Anyone who takes the time to examine his life can see the quiet hand of destiny making connections, arranging encounters, fulfilling long-held desires, bringing out inspirations and ideas from within. And now we are coming to know that this 'destiny' is nothing other than our own Self, our consciousness. In Maharishi's words, 'man now controls the trends of time'. By learning to use the deepest levels of our own awareness it seems that anything can be achieved: the entire accomplishment of the techno-logical age, all the achievements of the past, can now be accomplished by a great new technology— that of consciousness.

Mair Fenn has performed a kind and motherly task—the task of telling in simple language and from personal experience how easy and delightful it can be to reach fulfilment in the state of enlight-enment. All who are suffering (and all who are not) have everything to gain from reading this book and acting on its simple advice; to contribute to the creation of an ideal society by becoming a fulfilled, creative and happy person—a citizen of the Age of Enlightenment.

Byron Rigby, M.B., B.S., M.R.C.Psych.,
Professor of Psychiatry,
Maharishi European Research University,
Seelisberg, Switzerland.

1   The Search

Transcendental Meditation, as taught by Maharishi Mahesh Yogi, is a natural technique for relaxing
that is so simple a child can do it and yet is so
profound in its effects that it has cured many
diseases which are nervous in origin. It is essentially
a self-help cure.

TM, as it is called for short, is the most widely
tested relaxing technique in the world. Basically
these tests explore three different areas. First, the
bodily changes that take place (such as blood
pressure, breath rate and brainwave patterns) while
the technique is being practised; secondly, the long
term effects on such disorders as insomnia, bron-
chial asthma, blood pressure, allergies, certain heart
disorders, migraine and other conditions caused by
an overload of stress. Thirdly, what might be termed the development of the full human potential.
These tests are designed to ascertain whether
people who start the technique do indeed begin to
feel happier, think more clearly, make decisions

more easily, worry less and have better mind/body co-ordination.

More than two hundred universities and hospitals have taken part in these tests and more than five hundred scientific papers have been published. Anyone who examines the published reports cannot fail to be impressed and to admit that the claims made by the TM Organisations appear to be valid.

Being a meditator of ten years standing and a TM teacher for five, I no longer seek confirmation in the scientific reports because every time I teach someone the technique, I have the evidence before my eyes. Sometimes the change is dramatic, such as that in one of my pupils who was suffering so acutely from insomnia that she was on the verge of a nervous breakdown. From the first instruction her sleep-pattern returned to normal with a concomitant change in her life style that needs no elaboration. Others, and this is the majority, find slight changes taking place from the beginning, such as an increase in energy and a decrease in anxiety, an ability to make decisions more easily and to be even tempered. As they continue the practice, so these trends deepen until harmony and self assurance are firmly established. Often these changes, which are signs that the nervous system is being restructured, are so subtle that the TM practitioner is unaware they are taking place until a situation occurs that draws his attention to the change. I remember an engraver friend of mine, who has been meditating for three years, telling me how he was working under pressure for several days in order to clear out a backlog of work, preparatory to taking his summer holidays. Finally his son exclaimed, 'Hey daddy, do you realise how much work you've done?' Only then was the engraver aware that he had completed a fortnight's work at his fastest pre-TM standard in three days.

How then does TM work? At the risk of over-simplifying, we might say that every man, woman and child in this modern world has too much stress in his nervous system. By stress we mean a chemical deposit in the tissues or a twisting of the nerves out of alignment. It is a physical malformation, not a mental one, and has been brought about by subjecting the body to conditions beyond its normal range. Stress can be caused by loud noises, working under pressure, bad news, anger, over-excitement,etc., and it can occur by watching a film or a television programme as much as by experience in life.

Now we know that rest relieves stress so if we assume—as tests have conclusively proved—that TM puts the body into a state of rest deeper than the deepest sleep, then this stress will be automatically released every time we meditate. Anyone whose system is heavily loaded will naturally take longer to eliminate it, although he will feel the benefits right from the start; while those whose systems are strong and healthy will experience expansion of heart and mind and improved mind/body co-ordination.

Stress has driven us to a dependance on pills that is frightening: we take pills to get us to sleep, pills to quieten our over-excited nervous systems, pills to combat depression, pills to kill pain and even pills to overcome the bad effects of other pills. None of these go to the source of the trouble; they only smother the symptoms. With TM, however, we become our own physicians and heal ourselves by going to the root of the problem—we get rid of stress in our systems by means of deep rest.

Stress is not only the 'killer' of the day, it is also the 'kill-joy'; it takes the happiness out of living and replaces it by a veneer of anxiety. Yet it only needs two things to effect a cure: a desire to learn the TM Technique and the will-power to sit down by oneself in a comfortable chair, morning and evening, and enjoy twenty minutes of deep rest. Nothing could be easier and no matter how tense the nervous system may be, there is one big factor which is not normally taken into account: nature is on our side waiting to help.

Anyone who gardens will have come across the classic situation where a mound of weeds has accidentally been left all winter long on top of a precious plant, choking the life out of it. When the weeds are removed the shoots can be seen, so white and distorted that the plant seems doomed. However, as soon as the sun and air get at it, a remarkable transformation takes place and within a few days, it is growing again with full vigour.

This analogy reveals clearly the two-ply nature of TM, two threads woven finely together. One I think of as silver, the healing process (the clearing of the weeds), and the other as gold, the subsequent growth to full potential, which I prefer to think of as a growing awareness of the Big Self, the Self that lies beyond the petty tyrannies of life. Most people are first attracted to TM by the silver thread and some never discover the gold, since they cure themselves of their ills, and having achieved their object, discontinue the practice before gaining the most worthy benefit of all.

It is sometimes said that within the sphere of every person's life lies a universal statement and so it is that, at this point, I propose to turn from the general to the particular, in the hope that anyone who starts the TM Technique for themselves will find mirrored in this personal story a universal image.

Fate sometimes plays curious tricks; we can suffer a traumatic experience like a car accident or the death of a close friend without any radical change taking place inside and then some trivial incident, something we do not even expect is going to make impact, can change our lives. One such triviality happened to me in the spring of 1967. Switching on the radio to listen to the news, I caught part of another programme lasting perhaps thirty seconds. Those thirty seconds were to change my whole way of thinking and behaving. A woman's voice said something like this:

TM is a simple technique for relaxing, in which we take our awareness to quieter areas of the mind until we go beyond the quietest and reach the silent state underlying everything. . .

I paid no attention at the time and switched to my news programme. Later, on leafing through the *Radio Times*, I noticed that I had heard part of a talk given by the International Meditation Society in which was mentioned, among other things, that transcendental meditation helped to cure all 'the nervous afflictions that assail modern man'.

Although, like many others, I suffered from several of these afflictions they were minor complaints of which I took little notice. Consequently the aspect of the talk that lingered on in my mind

16

was 'the silent area underlying everything'. Being a Celt, a race noted for its pre-occupation with the inner life, I had always been interested in that 'silent area', particularly since I had been brought up without a religion. My mother, who was rebellious, had always said we would learn more about God on a mountain than in a chapel. In 1920 in a narrow Welsh mining valley where every other street was punctuated by bleak little chapels with names like Nebo and Ebeneezer, this was blasphemy.

My poet brother Alun Lewis called this inner preoccupation by another name:

My sister has always desired to be herself
Like a young foal or a lonely seagull
When the wind is wild on the sea-pastures.
She too has dreamed of darkness.

But whether it is called a dream or a preoccupation, the effect is the same: life becomes a quest.

In the 1930s intellectual rebels turned to atheism but I always thought this inconsistent. My father used to tell a story about a theologian and an atheist visiting a natural history museum. They came upon a working model of the solar system with all the planets moving in their orbits round the sun. The atheist was particularly struck by it and admired it from all angles.

'Incredible,' he exclaimed, 'such a sense of beauty... and so cleverly worked out. I wonder who made it?'

'No one,' replied the theologian and at the startled look on the atheist's face, he laughed. 'Well, that's what you say about the Universe.'

This still did not answer the question: who made the solar system? So I became an agnostic, ready to accept any answer that seemed logical. Thinking that a minister might be able to help, I attended a chapel where the preacher was young and lively but I soon discovered that he was teaching a moral code to those who already believed, or professed to believe or simply went to chapel because they liked the singing. For those who were seeking, he had no precepts to point the way to the infinite within.

The best that he could do was to murmur: 'Seek and ye shall find.'

Not long after this I went to live in London, and looking there, I found a variety of promising teachings. Buddhism was the first to interest me since belief in God was not an essential starting point and it offered meditation as a technique for self-exploration. However, in order to learn the technique. it was necessary to join the Buddhist Society. I hesitated: some of the dogma, such as reincarnation, or transmigration of souls, seemed foreign to me, as I did not even know whether I possessed a soul. But what finally prevented me from becoming a Buddhist was the precept that only by overcoming all desires of the flesh could you realise the full spiritual self. The Presbyterian minister's 'Seek and ye shall find' had been unhelpful but at least it was not anti-life. To quell desire seemed tantamount to shutting off the sap rising in the tree. As far as nature was concerned this was the way to distort a plant not enrich it, and man was subject to the same basic laws. Besides, I did not think I was capable of such rigid and concentrated self-denial, so I passed by this great religion with regret since there was much that I like about the teaching.

Next I read a book about the mystic teacher Gurdjieff whose doctrines were being taught in London. His theory was that although we thought we were individuals ruling our own destinies, we were in reality nothing by automatons reacting in a purely mechanical fashion to external stimuli and that, while this blind identification was taking place, our true selves slept. Escape from this dilemma was only possible by an effort of will. He recommended the creation of an observer, who was constantly watching the behaviour of his own automaton: he would then see that he was composed of innumerable 'I's'. There was the 'I' who talked down to his wife, the 'I' who showed off in front of the office girls, the 'I' who was obsequious to the boss. Every new situation called forth automatically a new 'I' and none of them was the real 'I'. Once the observer had realised the truth of this situation he was on the road to self-knowledge.

To observe oneself reacting automatically I found easy enough, but to keep my observer awake at his post at all times called for intense concentration. After several weeks I knew it was beyond my powers and I gave up.

My next involvement was even less orthodox. I became friends with a group of people who were trying to find 'The Way'. At the centre of the group was a man called Max who was said to be operating from his real 'I', his unbounded self. This situation came about like this: he and his wife Theta had just returned from a journey through Mexico in an ancient Land Rover. It was in the days before the North-South Highway had been built and he had followed the tracks of bullock carts. Once when boulders had blocked his route he had worked all day in the tropical sun digging them out and thus pushed himself beyond endurance. He fell into a coma which lasted for several days. On awakening he was aware of knowledge flooding into him, including a formula as simple as the famous Relativity Theory $E=mc^2$ and equally as profound though few could interpret its meaning.

When applied for instance to a motor car engine, it could simplify it to such an extent that the whole car industry would in consequence be revolutionised. Max approached the Ford Motor Company who were certainly interested but I imagine they could not decide whether he was a genius or a madman. His philosophy however made sense to me.

He claimed that we did not live fully in the 'Moment-Now' but that the major part of our attention was either in the future or the past: worries about what might happen, frustrations about what had not happened, day dreams, angers, dozens of neurotic preoccupations caused us to see the present as through a glass darkly. If instead we were to focus our whole attention on this moment which was part of a vast time-space continuum, what richness would we then experience.

Max and Theta were returning to Mexico to set up a school of philosophy in the jungle. When they invited me to go with them I felt too intrigued to refuse. The fact that none of us had any money was of little significance since it was an integral part of their philosophy that when you were searching on a spiritual level, the physical means automatically appeared. And indeed the money did come, as and when it was needed.

Things were always rather tough: my bed across the front seats of the Land Rover was too short for me to stretch out and as it was too hot to close the windows, millions of mosquitoes attacked my face nightly. At one point we were so hungry that Theta fainted several times. But when things were at their worst, a young Mexican came up to the camp with a present of a huge bunch of bananas. Through stifling heat, attacks of dysentry and moods of deep despair I clung to the fleeting 'Moment-Now' until at last I realised that it was like trying to pin down the flight of a butterfly.

When I returned to England on my thirty-eighth birthday, a man I had been friendly with for ten years quite unexpectedly asked me to marry him and I did so.

Bernard Shaw once wrote an allegory entitled *A Black Girl in Search of Her God* in which he described how intensely she looked everywhere for this great reality and finally found it in the shape of a man. In my 'liberated' frame of mind I despised such a concept but now found that this was precisely what happened to me. After two children were born, my preoccupation with the imponderables ceased.

These close relationships might have quietened my spiritual needs had I not taken a smear test and found that I was a cancer suspect. The shock of finding myself alone in the midst of a loving circle threw me back upon the old questions: who am I?

Who made the solar system? Life was short and death was for ever.

It was then that I remembered the radio talk on transcendental meditation: the voice had made it sound as if it were easy to journey to that silent area underlying everything. Perhaps TM was what I had always been looking for.

2 Unearthing the Treasure

At this time I was living on the west coast of Ireland, remote from any city where a technique such as TM might be taught. However, I found an advertisement of the International Meditation Society, giving a London address, to which I wrote.

The first page of the pamphlet that arrived a week later barely mentioned the mystical side and dealt mainly with the practical benefits you might expect if you started the practice, such as a cure for insomnia and a freedom from anxiety. This certainly gladdened my heart since I would wake at four o'clock every morning wondering if the hysterectomy I had undergone had in fact eliminated the cancer. I would then lie awake chasing these negative thoughts round and round in my mind until it was time to get up. This was one reason why I felt so enervated, and here again the pamphlet was quite definite in its statement: lack of energy would vanish. Could it cure osteo-arthritis too, I wondered, since I could no longer turn my neck freely and nodules were appearing on my finger joints, but this it did not mention.

The second page dealt with five points concerning the technique and these again held significance for me. First, no concentration was necessary and it was so easy that even a child could do it. How hard I had tried to live in the 'Moment-Now' and I had worked even harder at observing myself behaving like an automaton. Second, no belief was necessary—one could be a sceptic without preventing it from working. How many times had dogma barred my way at the outset of a quest? Third, there was no need for any change in one's life-style. TM simply gave deep rest which enabled the nervous system to throw off accumulated stresses and resulted in the establishment of harmony. In other words, happiness was to be enjoyed in *this* life, not in some vague hereafter in which I scarcely believed. Fourth, it was not necessary to join the society and attend meetings. How could I have done so, living as I did on a remote peninsula? Once the technique had been learned from a qualified teacher, you got on with it in your own home. And fifth, it only took twenty minutes night and morning sitting comfortably in an arm chair. It seemed too good to be true.

The last page dealt with the origin of the teaching. It came from the Vedic Tradition, which was almost as old as man himself and the knowledge of the technique had been handed down from one teacher to another through the ages. The last custodian was a renowned India sage called Swami Brahmananda Saraswati, or Guru Dev. Before he died he asked his closest disciple to bring the knowledge out into the world. This disciple, Maharishi Mahesh Yogi, was the founder of the International Meditation Society (IMS) and, from his photograph on the back page, looked about fifty, very benign and smiling.

Included with the pamphlet was the address of the Irish secretary, Mr Desmond Hourie, who was also the commercial superintendent to the Royal Dublin Society, but when I wrote to Mr Hourie he told me there was only one person in Ireland qualified to teach the technique and he was a sea captain constantly plying the high seas between Dublin and North Africa. Nearly a year went by and I still had not arranged a meeting with Captain Byrne when a second letter arrived from Mr Hourie giving me an address in Courtmacsherry, not sixty miles from my home, where an English TM teacher had come to live.

John Holmes had retired to Ireland to grow lilies and had chosen an isolated house overlooking the sea, far from the demands of civilisation; but such are the needs of our present day society that by the time I reached his front door, a dozen university students were already there. One of them had been experimenting with drugs and I remember being impressed by the teacher's firm yet understanding attitude. He first elicited the fact that the student was not satisfied with his life and was looking for a deeper meaning than any offered him in home and university and church, and this was why he had turned to drugs.

'You had good experiences with them?' John asked.

' 'Twas good all right,' the student agreed. 'Bright swirling patterns of colour and feeling at one with with everything but after a bit I had some bad experiences and now they're mostly bad, only it's difficult to stop.'

'TM will help you there,' John said. 'They've found in the States that a large percentage, something like ninety percent, stop taking drugs when they start TM because you not only get good experiences but you can hang on to them too. Mind you, it's not an overnight cure. It's slow and gradual and what is more—I can't do it for you, I can only give you the technique—you must have the self-discipline to build it into the routine of your life. Think you can?'

The lad nodded. 'I'll have a good try anyway.'

I was one of the last to learn and I watched curiously as the others returned one by one to the room, their eyes bright, their faces softer and not saying a word about their experiences. At last my turn came and I was led into a small room at the back of the house where John performed in Sanscrit a ceremony of thanksgiving to the teachers who had kept this knowledge alive. Then very softly and with a minimum of explanation he gave me the technique. Almost immediately I felt myself sinking into a state of deep relaxation and although I was aware of everything going on in the room, none of the sounds penetrated the cocoon of stillness that enfolded me. From this first innocent experience I knew that the 'silent state underlying everything' really did exist. When I got home I eagerly waited for my evening meditation, meaning to visit that fulfilling quietness once more. Alas, thoughts, thoughts, and more thoughts pervaded my meditation, bubbling up from nowhere in their usual neurotic fashion.

Bitterly disappointed I rang John up the next day. 'I can't do it.'

'Can't do what?'

'Get to that silent area.'

'That's not the purpose of the practice,' he said sternly. 'The whole practice is meant to be easy and natural. We don't try in any way, we simply let nature do all the work.'

Three times I made the journey to Courtmacsherry before John was satisfied that the practice was flowing easily. He also explained exactly how the system worked and why our eight hours in bed were no longer sufficient to keep our nervous system functioning smoothly:

There are two nervous systems in the body: the automatic and the reticular. The automatic, for the most part, acts without direction from the brain—the heart goes on beating and the stomach digesting without continually being told to and if a virus attacks this system an automatic reaction is set in motion to push the foreign bodies out, such as sneezing in a cold or sweating it out as in a fever. This mechanism operates best when the body is at rest, which is why we go to bed to cure ourselves of illness. Exactly the same thing happens with the reticular nervous system, only that deals with the day's events—a blow, a startling sight, can leave a foreign deposit behind and these stresses have to be eliminated before smooth functioning can take place. Just as the automatic nervous system eliminates the virus when in a state of rest, so does the reticular system. But, this is where the problem arises. . . our nervous systems have been inherited, relatively unchanged, from primitive man and the events he passed through in a day—up with the dawn, digging the garden, milking the cows, bed at sunset—were easily eliminated in his night's sleep. Not so with our day which might include a hair-raising drive to work, a painful interview with the boss, or eating a rich lunch and trying to pull off a business contract at the same time. Typical situations that overload the system to such an extent that a back-log of stress begins to build up. What is needed in the present day is not longer in bed but a deeper quality of rest.

Throughout nature, he said, we could see the same pattern of rest and activity: there was night and day, winter's rest, followed by the rapid growth of spring. The deeper the rest, the more powerful the activity was nature's law, and he concluded with these words:

'In TM of course you get a deeper rest even than in the deepest sleep.'

'How do you know that?'

He looked surprised that I should ask such a question. 'Because breathing stops, of course, and it never does that in sleep.'

'You mean that breathing stops altogether?' I asked in alarm.

'Naturally.'

His wife gave me a reassuring pat on the shoulder. 'Don't worry. John's been meditating many years and he thinks everyone has the same experience as himself.'

'It won't take long before you do,' John said. 'And another thing. You'll be getting a news letter from the TM people later this month telling you about residential courses. I suppose that with two small children it will be difficult for you to get away but they really are excellent.'

It was not only the two small children that made the courses out of the question, but money. My husband is a writer and all writers, except the lucky 'best-selling' few, are unlikely to earn as much as a dustman. But a thoughtful writer understands the need for evolution and expansion, not only for himself but also for his wife. Although he did not learn TM himself, my husband always encouraged me as much as he could.

As with most mothers, my waking hours were devoted to the needs of the family and it seemed strange at first to go off into a room by myself for my twenty minutes' TM when I had already had my quota of sleep. But it was the beginning of a liberation, a time to find my 'self', and it had its repercussions on the rest of the family. With the uncanny insight common to most children, mine quickly discovered that although I might be irritable when I went off to do my practice I would always emerge cheerful and happy, so they rarely disturbed me. It was in relation to the children that I first noticed definite changes taking place. Where once their noisy play had occasionally reduced me to tears, partly because of the noise but partly because I felt they were doing it on purpose to annoy, now my equilibrium was unshakable and I realised that their noise was simply the bubbling up of an energy that could not be suppressed. This capacity to see things differently had the same effect as fitting a wide angled lens to a camera; with the wider vision, the character of the scene changed. If for instance my husband spoke irritably to me I realised that the basic cause of his anger was tension set up by a completely different chain of circumstances: knowing this, the sting went out of the situation.

A general sense of well-being began to pervade my days. I was sleeping better, feeling stronger, and that cloak of debility and anxiety I had been wearing for years was gradually disappearing.

About this time I read *Erewhon* written by Samuel Butler in 1901 in which he described the law of a strange country he visited in his imagination:

> . . . if a man falls ill, or catches any disorder, or fails bodily in any way before he is seventy years old, he is tried before a jury of his countrymen, and if convicted is held up to public scorn. . . a man being punished very heavily for serious illness, while failure of eyes or hearing in one over

sixty-five is dealt with by fine only.

In the light of TM, this seemingly ridiculous law is not so preposterous. Most doctors think that seventy per cent of all illnesses are psychosomatic—the nervous system is not functioning properly. Because of the pressure of modern life, an overload of stress is the most common cause of this malfunction. The cure of stress problems is rest, deep rest. But part of the difficulty is that when the system has become overloaded in this way, it will not switch off, except by artificial means such as tranquillisers and sleeping pills, neither of which do any deep-seated good and may even do harm. So if there were a foolproof way of putting the body naturally into a state of deep rest, seventy per cent of all illnesses could be cured by the sufferers themselves. According to Samuel Butler's thesis, anyone who did not avail themselves of this opportunity but continued to inflict their nervous torments on others ought to be tried before a jury.

Although I knew that TM was giving me deep rest, my own subjective experiences were of little use in convincing others. When I first started to tell people how much better I felt as a result of the practice, I saw an embarrassed look appear on their faces and they would invariably change the subject. Gradually I realised that they thought I had been converted to some queer religion and felt sorry for me.

In cities, of course, the pressure of living drives people to enquire about such techniques but in country places people tend to shy away from anything new like TM for fear of being laughed at. It is of course easy to dismiss a personal statement as wishful thinking but scientific proofs cannot be so easily dismissed and I longed for external verification of what was happening inside me.

In the spring of the following year, 1969, a news letter came from the International Meditation Society advertising several courses. The one that attracted me most was two weeks in Lancaster University at a cost of £40.00 (pre-inflation). It was, of course, out of the question for me to attend on our limited income and with the children still only six and eight, but I remembered my journey to Mexico in search of the 'Moment-Now' and the way nature had always sustained me. Would it not do the same now?

The idea of the Lancaster course persisted in my mind so I began to move in the direction I wanted to go—I made inquiries about someone to look after the children. . . effected economies. . . borrowed a little. . . talked the matter over once more with my husband. Within a few weeks it was all planned and for the first time since my marriage ten years previously I set out on my own, feeling very unsure of myself. Would the other participants in the course be young and noisy and make me feel old? I need not have worried. Although the majority were in their twenties, with equal numbers of both sexes, mostly university students, they were so relaxed and easy in manner that I was hardly aware of the disparity in our ages.

All had different stories to tell about how TM had helped them but the one I remember most vividly came from a woman about my own age. She was unhappily married and doted on her one child, a daughter. When this daughter wanted to marry, she opposed it because she could not bear the thought of losing her. Finally, after a quarrel, the daughter walked out and got married. Still the mother kept pleading with them to share the house, which finally drove the daughter to live in a distant town. In despair the mother turned to TM and within a few months became centred and stable within herself. Her emotional dependence on her daughter vanished and now that the couple were not constantly being importuned, they came to visit her every other weekend of their own volition and all were very happy together.

The course, as John had said, was admirable. On the first day we were taught some Yoga exercises and some pranayama (breathing exercises) to which we added our twenty minutes TM. This was called a 'round' and we did enough of these rounds in a day to keep our metabolism low so that deep rooted stresses would be released. This stress release was experienced as an occasional headache, irritability, or roughness, followed by periods of deepening quietness and harmony.

There were also lectures explaining how the TM Technique worked from A to Z. The theory hinged on the supposition that there existed within each one of us an area termed the Source of Thought. Pragmatically I knew that this existed, having experienced it during the practice, but for someone lacking this experience I felt that the theory would be less convincing. It was, however, simple enough to understand.

If we observe the force of nature at work in the external world we can see that it operates in a harmonious and orderly fashion. Even when we observe it functioning on a colossal scale, such as with the planets orbiting over vast spaces, we find that, from an observer post on earth, their points of intersection can be calculated hundreds of years in advance with split second accuracy. If we examine a snowflake we will see the same exquisitely balanced order reflected in its crystalline structure. Or if we look through a high powered electronic microscope we see even on the minutest level the same harmonious and orderly force at work. Now this same force is functioning in every cell of our bodies and each thought that we think. Many of these thoughts we express in words, which means that they move from within to without. Now anything that moves has energy inherent in it and anything that moves in a particular direction must have intelligence guiding it; therefore thoughts have these two inherent qualities—energy and intelligence. As there are thousands of thoughts arising within us in the course of a day, it means that somewhere within lies a source of energy and intelligence; we call this the Source of Thought, or sometimes it is referred to as the Souce of Creative Intelligence.

The channel is there since we are using it continuously whenever thoughts come into our minds and TM is simply a technique for reversing this process. We take our attention from the most gross form of a thought (that is, the spoken word) back through more and more refined levels until we come to the most refined, nor do we stop there but go beyond (the word transcend simply means 'go beyond') the finest level to an area of 'no thought'. We are still aware but we have no thoughts.

What continued to puzzle me in spite of this explanation was the claim that the natural tendency of the mind took us automatically to the Souce of Thought. It seemed to me that the natural

.tendency of my mind was always directed outwards, but this too was satisfactorily explained in the following manner.

The famous scientist, priest and writer Teilhard de Chardin begins an essay on happiness with these words:

> In the world of mechanised matter, all bodies obey the laws of a universal gravitation; similarly, in the world of vitalised matter, all organised beings, even the very lowest, steer themselves and progress towards that quarter in which the greatest measure of well-being is to be found.

Maharishi calls this natural law, when operating in man, the desire for more and more. What this amounts to in practical terms is that if you place a plate of roast beef, some matchbox cars and a Leonardo painting in a room and then you usher in a small boy, a hungry man and an artist. The boy will automatically make for the cars, the hungry man for the food and the artist will gravitate to the painting. Now the TM Technique creates a situation in which the mind and the Source of Thought are placed, as it were, in the same room and as this vast reservoir of energy and intelligence is so fulfilling in its nature, no matter whether the mind belongs to a child or an artist or a hungry man, it will automatically move towards it.

The lecturer then went on to explain that it is

difficult to observe this natural tendency of the mind at work, since the brain is a highly complex computer constantly receiving a stream of data through the five senses, codifying it and sending out directives in an ever-changing environment. Consequently the mind is always on the move from one thought to another. It can be likened to a bee flitting from flower to flower. A casual observer might think the nature of the bee was always to be changing from one thing to another, whereas the quest of the bee is constant—nectar. Similarly the mind, though constantly moving, is seeking one thing only—its own well-being or, as Maharishi would say, more and more until it arrives at the most, the transcendent.

'How can you experience the transcendent if you have no thought?' someone asked. 'To experience this no-experience must be a thought in itself.'

The lecturer took this in his stride. 'You're aware of a feeling of stillness and harmony but you don't register it until you come out,' he said. 'That's why in the beginning people often have a very hazy experience of it.'

Sometimes I have found it difficult to relate the description of the mechanics to what I experienced subjectively while I was doing it, but I supposed it was like comparing the onset of measles, such as a headache and sore throat, to a description a doctor might give of what the microbes and viruses were doing. But I did clearly recognise the Transcendent state he referred to as it has occurred to me at infrequent intervals. Often I went for weeks at a time feeling only relatively quiet and sometimes I spent the entire twenty minutes with my head full of thoughts. This too the lecturer explained in lucid terms.

'The main purpose of TM is not to get to the T state but to release all the stress in the system. And finally, when you've cleared out every last bit, the silent T state becomes a permanent built-in feature of the mind.'

'How long does it take?' someone asked.

'It depends upon the state of your nervous system when you begin and the number of rounding programmes you do, but it'll take a good few years. It's the first stage on the path to self-knowledge, called Cosmic Consciousness, and it means that the force of nature, or Creative Intelligence as we call it, is flowing smoothly through your system without encountering any stress to distort its flow into anger or other life-destroying actions. In return, everything you do will get the support of nature. In big things you'll find that whatever you want to achieve seems to flow towards you. In little things, like your wanting to phone someone, they phone you instead—or if you want a particular coloured sweater someone will give it to you without your saying anything.'

'Would you say that this is just confined to people who do TM?'

'Not at all. It applies to anyone who is evolving. The way Maharishi puts it is that evolution is more important to life than existence is. What he means is that if you're evolving towards higher states of consciousness, the things you need for that expansion will come to you automatically, but if you're simply trying to keep your body alive, to get it food and clothing, life will just be a grim struggle.'

As the course came to an end I had an experience which made a very powerful impression upon me. Towards the end of the morning's meditations I was suddenly transported into another world: my body seemed to vanish and I found myself in a vast plane of nothingness. I too was nothing, not even a dot in that nothingness, but instead of desolation, thankfulness and relief flooded through me because I felt as if I had arrived home after an arduous journey. This experience lasted no more than a few seconds but it was very vivid and for the whole of that day filled me with serene happiness while my body seemed extraordinarily light and buoyant. I told the lecturer about it, expecting him to be impressed, but he explained that we do not take any notice of subjective experiences as they are simply signposts on the road to total release of stress.

I returned home more convinced than ever that TM was taking me along the path I wished to pursue but unable to convince anyone else, including my family, that it was a practical technique for living.

Tolstoy once wrote to his wife: '. . . the inner life of any human is a secret between himself and God and no one else can call him to account in any way.'

It was not that I wanted to keep it a secret but that I could not find the right words to convince them.

As it was mid-July and the tourist season was just beginning, the first practical thing I did was to paint a sign that read 'Bed and Breakfast' which my husband put up in the garden. Before August was out I had paid back the money borrowed for the course, not, I must confess, without some smug feelings on the subject of 'nature support'.

Indeed this means of paying for courses was so pleasant and brought so many interesting people into our lives—people from all over the world, who came as strangers and left as friends—that it grew into a way of life and expanded into the building of a small Arts Centre on the sea's edge where we provide easels and desks and typewriters to creative people who want a congenial place to work.

Since the tourist season lasts only two months, my husband and I can devote the other ten months to our own creative pursuits including my own efforts at painting and making jewelry.

3   The World Plan

In the spring of 1971 a news letter came from the International Meditation Society advising me that there would be a three week course in Austria in the autumn which Maharishi himself would attend. If I wished to go it would be as well to book early. I was naturally curious to see the person who offered happiness in this life in an easy effortless way. After three years of TM during which I had hardly missed a sitting, I could vouch for the truth of the second statement and the first also seemed to be manifesting itself more and more as time went on. As for the 'support of nature' that was said to accompany progress towards higher states of consciousness, this was certainly becoming evident. Some people might of course put it down to coincidence that, although my husband and I still devoted our main energies towards creativity, regardless of whether it had commercial value or not, there was now a margin of spare money for us all: my husband to do some research for a book in

London, the children to stay with friends and I to set off for the beautiful Austrian village of Kossen.

There were several thousand people on this course; every country in Europe was represented and many from the Americas. As the majority arrived by the same train there were long queues at the desks where our papers were checked and accommodation given out. It took the best part of three hours and yet in all that time there was not a murmur of anger and everyone was so softly spoken, so gentle and friendly that it was almost a pleasure to go through such an ordeal after a journey lasting two days and nights!

My *pension* was several miles up the mountainside and looked out across the fields to a large wooden farmstead and towering mountains. It was on this course that I began to lose my 'middle-aged spread' without even trying. With a small camping gas cooker, I lived mostly on soup and dairy products and had a mountain climb three times a day as well as six sets of Yoga exercises. It made me very fit and flexible.

The lecture hall, in the middle of the village, was very modern and seated about two thousand people. I arrived early the next morning and, putting my jacket and notebook on a front seat, went to wait in the sunshine for the arrival of Maharishi. Long skirts were in fashion and there

were several lovely long-haired, long-skirted girls
sitting on a wall, each with a rose in her hand. When
I remarked on their flowers, they explained that it
was a present for Maharishi, a mark of respect. It
struck me that I already owed him a lot of respect
for the changes that were coming into my life so I
went looking for a florist. The roses were exorbi-
tantly expensive but the price I owed was beyond
pearls, so I decided to cut out lunch and chose a
rose with a soft flame colour. When I returned I
saw the long-skirted girls walking towards the back
entrance of the hall while everyone else was throng-
ing excitedly in through the main doors as if
Maharishi were expected at any moment. Joining
the others at the back of the car park, I felt a little
nervous: if I disliked him, would it put me off TM?
Could anything put me off TM? The few news-
paper articles I had read about him had been anta-
gonistic: 'What does he do with the initiation
money?' they asked. 'How many Rolls Royces
does he have?' I was therefore expecting at least a
Cadillac or a Bentley so that when a shabby blue
car appeared, driven by a pleasant-faced woman of
about my age, I did not even look at the passenger
in the front seat until the vehicle stopped right
under my nose. Then I saw a very exotic looking
figure dressed in white silk, with flowing black hair
and a long white beard. The girl next to me opened

the door, a small sandalled foot appeared, then out stepped Maharishi, his stature in keeping with that small foot and his modesty in keeping with that stature. He carried a bouquet of carnations and sweet peas and looked more like a bride going to her wedding than a guru arriving for a lecture. The girl offered Maharishi her rose and then I offered mine. He took it with a smile and then passed up the steps into the hall. Whey was there a sudden gush of tears to my eyes? Was it because he seemed so vulnerable?

Whatever it was, I did not stop to analyse but raced round to the front of the hall and reached my seat in time to sec him slip off his sandals and sit crosslegged on a couch facing us. He did not give set lectures but answered questions and there was always a long line of Course Participants at the microphone. Even before he had finished answering the first question I realised that for the first time in my life I was in the presence of a seer. Every question, no matter how complex (and there was a physicist there who asked questions of incredible complexity) he answered with a simplicity that satisfied both the expert and the amateur. Indeed, one of his first dissertations was based on the different approach to a problem exhibited by an expert and an amateur. When a cog in a machine gets broken, he told us, the amateur will go and buy another cog and replace it. The expert, however, will examine the whole machine to see why the cog broke and then go to the root of the trouble to set it right. Maharishi told us that with the aid of TM we would soon become experts in living.

Someone asked him a question about love and marriage and he talked at some length in a quiet gentle voice:

The nature of life is love. You can't take love from life or from self. Love is unifying. Wherever there is love there is greater happiness. No one can remain shut off from a person who loves because love is boundless and only a restricted vision prevents us from experiencing love in this way. If you love someone as yourself then it has meaning. You love yourself not because you are five feet tall; you love yourself because you can't be without yourself. Love is purity and if it's not purity, it's nothing. A mother loves her child for no reason. If he's blind she loves him; if he has two eyes—fine. Three eyes? She still loves him. That is the child and that is the mother, and what holds them together is love. Married life has to be the same; when both give then both receive. Always giving, always yes to the husband; always yes to the wife. The only thing between them is yes. Yes binds the two into one. Love knows no reason; he loves his wife because he loves her; she loves her husband because she loves him. If there is a reason for loving—if he loves her gold hair—that reason may disappear; if love depends on a situation then it's going to be over very soon. People who hate themselves hate their wives and hate everything. Hate comes from stress; when stress is strong in society then hate is the basic platform of life and this is not good.

He had an irresistible sense of humour and kept us all chuckling. It was rumoured and later confirmed that he only slept about three hours at night: the light in his hotel room usually went out from three to six. Then, as now, he was carrying the whole movement along, making all decisions down to the finest details. As he never hurried and dealt with everything as it came into his orbit, with his full attention, this made the timetable erratic. Evening lectures were scheduled from nine to eleven but frequently he would not arrive until midnight and then would talk until two or three in the morning. His whole approach to life was spontaneous: more than anyone I had ever met, he lived exclusively in the 'Moment-Now' and had the capacity to carry everyone else along with him. One night, in the middle of a lecture, he paused and looked around.

'Is it not full moon tonight?' Everyone chorused

that it was and his face lit up. 'Would it not be nice to go up into the mountains and admire the moonlight?' On hearing the hum of delight that greeted his remark he rose to his feet. 'Let us go—there are enough cars, yes?'

There were about four hundred cars parked outside and with a minimum of fuss, everyone streamed out of the hall and into the cars as if it had been organised beforehand. Within fifteen minutes a long line of cars was making its way to a plateau high up in the mountains where, sitting on the grass, we had a group meditation before going back to our hotels.

Two days later I saw another example of this unorganised but orderly flow which was more dramatic. Across the valley from my *pension* was a huge wooden farmstead where the hay, the cattle and the people were all housed under the same large roof. As I walked home from the morning lectures, I saw a wisp of smoke rise up from the barn. With all that dry timber and hay, I knew there was going to be a conflagration and I began to run for help. Within five minutes the flames were roaring into the sky, the fire engine squealing to a stop and the church bells pealing for help. The ones who answered the bells were the meditators: like a surging river they came rushing up the hill and across the fields. The farmer himself had rescued the livestock and his little family was standing in a corner of the field struck dumb with shock. By the time the meditators reached the farm, the roof timbers were aflame and chunks of burning wood were falling into the interior. Heedless of the danger some of the young men ran in through the open door and began handing out chairs and crockery and clothing. The rest of the men clustered around the doors and windows to take the objects and handed them to the girls who, by this time, had found an empty garage nearby. I saw one of the young meditators, whom I knew well galloping up the stairs to appear at the window with a pillow which he flung down to those waiting below.

As I hurried back and forth with homely objects, such as chamber pots and broken toys, I kept muttering to myself. 'It's worthless, all worthless... why don't they get out?'

Miraculously they did, before the heavy roof timbers collapsed with a mighty roar, and by that time everything had been saved: all those objects worth so little in themselves that when put together, make up a home. The meditators had accomplished the task with the same co-ordinated efficiency as a hive of bees at work.

Having lived through several war years in London when buzzbombs were constantly falling out of the sky, I had experienced the heart warming effect of people being drawn together by common danger, but this was different. It is often said that the whole is greater than the sum of the parts, but it was the first time I had been aware of the greatness of the whole and I was glad to have been a drop in the flow that had as its underlying principle the common good of men.

By the end of the three weeks a conviction had formed in my mind, which subsequent events have only served to strengthen, that Maharishi is going to change the pattern of man's behaviour in this generation. Up until then I had always believed that people could not change the behaviour patterns dictated by their natures. What I had not taken into account was how stress could distort that nature and thus the behaviour patterns.

It is this distortion I think that accounts for modern man's fall from grace. Experts in ecology, sociology, psychology and economy tell us that either there must be a change of heart or man will so pollute himself and the world that the balance of nature will be destroyed by the turn of the century—the end is in sight.

Whenever I read one of these doomsday books I have a vision of that burning farmhouse and the living chain of figures, only now instead of saving household goods, they are restoring harmony to the world. After all, man is destroying the bàlance of his environment only because he himself is not balanced. Intrinsically the solution is simple—too simple perhaps for some people to believe its efficacy. It only needs enough people free from stress, working in unison within that orderly nature force, for the problems of the world to vanish and this transformation is in my opinion already taking place at a much more rapid rate than is generally realised. It is easy to observe anger and fear spreading throughout the world since the papers are full of it. But harmony is ignored—good news is no news, yet it is pervading the atmosphere in an invisible fashion.

There are now more than a thousand cities and towns in the world where one per cent of the population is doing TM. This figure of one per cent is of great significance since it has been discovered that when one in every hundred of the population is doing TM, their influence begins to spread over the whole community. Extensive tests have been done on this subject and the results are conclusive: as a general rule in all major cities accident and crime rates continue to soar; in cities where the 'Maharishi Effect' is taking place, they are dropping. Thus when a city's anger is defused the quality of life improves for everyone.

The growth rate of the TM Organisation when

measured over a ten year period in the States, was discovered to be between a hundred and a hundred and fifty per cent, making it the fastest growing organisation in the world, with more than two million people practising the technique. The reason for its rapid growth is that much of it is done by personal recommendation: one person convinces three of his friends that it is good, the three friends convince nine of their friends, the nine convince twenty-seven, the twenty-seven convince eighty-one, the eighty-one convince two hundred and forty-three and so on.

Far from being a doomsday man, Maharishi is a supreme optimist. He declared that 1975 was the Dawn of the Age of Enlightenment and with 14,000 teachers teaching the technique, he has every reason to be pleased with the progress he is making in defusing the anger of the world.

4 Becoming a Teacher

When I returned from the Kossen course I was so
full of enthusiasm for the teaching that I wanted to
reach the widest possible audience. As a beginning
I arranged to give a talk in our Arts Centre. Several
days before a TV team had arrived at our door saying they would like to do a programme on the Arts
Centre. To my delight they not only included the
talk on TM but gave it ten minutes peak viewing
time. This type of 'coincidence' is sometimes
referred to in the movement as 'skill in action',
that is, getting maximum results from minimum
effort. It becomes an increasingly accepted part of
one's daily activity due to the fact that as we dip
constantly deeper into more refined areas of the
mind, we tend to act from this expanded area, and
the more refined the level we work from, the more
powerful it becomes.

Whenever a TM news letter came I read it eagerly. To become a teacher took two and a half
months and cost £500. Neither presented insuper-

able difficulty with nature to support me, I thought optimistically, but I was not quite getting that kind of support yet, so I continued on my way.

In the next two years the movement began to expand rapidly. Mr Desmond Hourie was made National Leader in 1971, a centre was opened in Eccles Street in Dublin and then another in Ailesbury Road. Three, four, five teachers became qualified in Ireland while on a world-wide scale the number of teachers grew from 200 in 1970 to 10,000 by 1975.

Finally in 1973 time and money came together for me. The children were both away in boarding school and my husband was leaving on a lecture tour to America. My teacher-training course took place in La Antilla on the south-west coast of Spain in the spring. There was no hall large enough to house the fifteen hundred people who had come for training and a vast blue canvas marquee was set up on the beach within the sound of the breakers rolling in from the Atlantic. We were housed in flats, one to a room, and fed in canteens run by meditators who were working their way through the teaching course. For the first time, concessions were make to the senior citizens over forty. They were given the best accommodation available and a small restaurant in which to eat. There were about fifty of us who thoroughly appreciated not having to queue at the two large restaurants on the water front.

In these two months I worked harder than at any other time in my life. At the age of fifty-two my ability to learn things off by heart had greatly deteriorated and there was a lot to learn: there was the procedure for teaching the technique and the long complicated framework for ensuring that people were meditating correctly. There were also two introductory talks to be prepared and three follow-up lectures, while the major portion of the day was spent in a 'rounding' programme of exercises and meditation. In order to get through the course I was up at 6.30 each morning and did not stop working until well after midnight. It now takes a minimum of two years to become a teacher and includes such practical training as how to run a centre, how to set up a symposium and how to make a presentation of the teaching to different professional bodies.

It was a La Antilla that I first heard about the scientific studies that had been carried out in England and America since 1965. Maharishi is himself a scientist, having taken a degree in physics in Allahabad University. From the beginning he took a great interest in the experiments and actively encouraged them.

The easiest and perhaps most conclusive test deals with breathing. As everyone knows who has run twenty yards, the more work your body does, the faster you breathe, that is, the more oxygen you take in. The reverse is also true: the deeper the degree of rest, the more shallow the breathing. Thus a person sitting down takes in less oxygen than a person walking about, while a person in the first stages of a sleep breathes even less. After about five hours sleep, the body is in a state of rest deeper than any during the twenty-four hours and the intake of oxygen is eight per cent below the intake during normal activity. However, a person starting his TM pactice almost immediately falls into a state of rest deeper even than this: the oxygen intake drops to an unprecedented sixteen per cent below that during normal activity. At the same time, the blood pressure drops, the heart beat slows by about five beats per minute indicating that the amount of blood pumped out decreases by about twenty-five per cent, confirming that the work load on the heart is being considerably reduced.

Another interesting aspect of the tests concerned the blood lactate level. It was found by experiment that when people were given an injection of lactate they became worried and anxious while a low lactate level was accompanied by feelings of stability and harmony. Now when people sat to do their TM practice the lactate level dropped as dramatically as the oxygen intake, that is by sixteen per cent, and although it did come back to its pre-TM norm, it took quite some time, showing that the effects of TM are taken over into activity.

Knowledge of these tests has now spread throughout the world and more and more hospitals and universities are carrying out experiments. A large bibliography now exists covering over three hundred tests carried out in more than one hundred institutions and over one hundred scientific papers on the TM Programme have been reprinted in full by the Maharishi European Research Unit Press.

Psychological tests have pointed to similar changes in other areas. It has been found that when students started doing TM they developed an increased ability to think more clearly, be more creative and their intelligence gowth rate increased.

On the level of personality, too, certain definite characteristics manifested themselves: students became more sure of themselves, developed inner directedness, a capacity for developing warm inter-personal relationships, self confidence, stability and balance.

Some of the most interesting tests were done with electroencephalograph machines which register, by means of electrodes taped to the head, the brain waves that are flowing through the different parts of the brain. In our normal waking state, the brain is receiving messages from all the senses at the same time, sorting the information and sending back replies in a rapidly changing world: this is very confusing and complex and it is not surprising that the different hemispheres of the brain do not work in synchrony; in fact all the brain waves are chaotic. Some nerve specialists think this lack of synchrony may be a bigger contributory factor than stress to the breakdown in mental health now manifesting itself throughout the world. During the practice of TM, as the awareness settles down to quieter areas of the mind, so also do the waves in both halves of the brain settle into alpha activity of large amplitude (indicating that the mind is in a state of deep relaxation). Not only do the two halves of the brain settle into this alpha activity but different areas of the scalp begin to follow the same pattern, indicating an overall sychrony of the whole brain. It now appears that this cohesion is responsible for improved athletic performance. Tennis players can hit the ball with greater accuracy when the impression received and the message sent are both 'on the same wave length'; athletes can run a fraction faster, leap a fraction higher or a fraction further which is all important in competitive athletics.

Dr B. C. Glueck, Director of Research at the

Hartford Institute of Living, a large psychiatric hospital in the USA, has put forward the theory that this silent, coherent state of mind and body experienced in TM is a fourth major state of consciousness. The other three are waking, dreaming and dreamless sleep, each with their own distinctive combinations of mental and physical features. In waking the body and mind are active. In dreamless sleep the body and mind are at rest. In dreaming, the body is at rest but the mind active. In the transcendent state there is the unusual combination of the body in a very deep state of rest while the mind is alert but almost inactive.

Until recently very little research had been done on the physiology of meditation since it was first necessary to find a yogi and then persuade him to undergo tests in a laboratory. Since TM has become so widespread, however, it is easy for hospitals and universities to carry out research programmes and, of course, doctors are earnestly looking for a natural cure against the ill of the day: stress.

The two and a half months spent on the west coast of Spain passed very quickly and as the teaching programme neared its end I wondered whether the Thanksgiving Ceremony, which was an integral part of the programme, was going to cause me any problems. Although I knew it was a simple ceremony of thanksgiving to the long line of teachers who had handed down this supreme knowledge, I had an inherent dislike of ceremony of any sort, thinking it to be a hollow show. But now I discovered its very real purpose—a means of maintaining the purity of the teaching.

Maharishi told us: 'Whether someone is learning in Hong Kong or Iceland, whether the teacher has a cold in the head or a fit of depression, makes no difference. Every word, every pause, every action is prescribed—there is no room for error.'

A very comforting thought but even so, when I left La Antilla I could not help wondering if I were really capable of passing on this gift of deep rest.

As soon as I could, I gave an introductory talk in the nearby market town of Skibbereen. Few people came to it since in 1973 TM was still relatively unknown in country places, and fewer still decided to learn the technique, but it was enough for me to realise that the magic inherent in TM was there waiting for anyone who wanted to make us of it.

One of the first people to start was a woman who had lived all her life in the country and had little education. A.C. of Skibbereen had been recently widowed and was trying to bring up three children on a widow's pension. To put it in her own words:

The first year I don't know how I went through
it. I walked round in circles with this terrible
load. I was also suffering from high blood
pressure and was on blood pressure tablets.

TM changed all this and her children (aged nine,
fourteen and sixteen), who were also in a 'state'
occasioned by their mother's distress, decided to
start the practice and gained immeasurably from it.
But, at the same time, I was concerned that A. C.
would not be able to understand the three follow-
up lectures which seemed to me quite complicated
but I soon discovered that the teaching was geared
for everyone. A. C. later wrote to me:

. . . I was only a short time doing TM when I
could find a great change in myself. I was sleeping very well. I was able to cope with my work. I
was no longer frightened or irritable. At the end
of three months my doctor was able to take me
off blood pressure tablets. . . A friend of mine
came visiting me three months ago, and for the
first time in four years I neglected my TM; as a
result my blood pressure went up, and I went to
the doctor. He put me back on blood pressure
tablets again for a month. As I returned to my
TM routine my blood pressure level dropped
once more.

As I gained experience in teaching I found it to
be even more creative than painting. Painting has

always been for me a means of communicating an inner experience for the enjoyment of others. TM is a means of communicating inner experience that enables them, as it were, to paint their own pictures, to evolve to their fullest potential without any further help. However the teaching does include further help for those who want it: a checking service is now available in all TM centres. We are so used to putting effort into anything we do that the same thing sometimes happens in TM, which hinders the practice. The checking is a simple procedure for reminding people that it is an effortless technique.

Five years ago there was only one TM centre in Ireland but now there are six. In the same period the number of TM teachers grew from one to thirty and the number of people who learned the technique increased to 10,000. Of this number there are two per cent in Sligo, one per cent in Tralee, one per cent in Carlow, one per cent in Galway and one per cent in my nearest market town of Skibbereen. Since the numbers practising the technique grow in geometric progression, we may expect these numbers to increase ever more rapidly in future.

The centres that have been set up in the cities not only ensure that everyone is meditating correctly but hold meetings once a week to discuss difficulties that may arise and to talk about the philosophy that lies behind the teaching. They also organise weekend residential courses for deepening the experiences. The checking programme and weekly meetings are both free, a fact that has established a strong feeling of confidence in the movement. TM is here to stay, its dedicated purpose to help restore the balance in the world by helping each individual to regain harmony within. A forest is green because every tree in the forest is green and in the same way, the world will become free of stress only when individuals themselves become free of stress. TM is the simplest way of achieving this.

There is now a seven-step programme for learning the technique taught every week in the centres. First come two introductory lectures (both of which are free and non-committal) telling of the ideas behind the technique. For those deciding to learn the technique there now comes a personal interview. Then follows the actual teaching of the technique and here also, each person is taught individually. Finally there are three follow-up lectures and these must be attended on the three subsequent evenings following the day of learning. After that, you can either attend weekly meetings and be checked as often as you wish, or you can get on with the practice yourself in your own home for the rest of your life without making any further TM contact. It does not matter which you do, the benefits will be the same.

As far as these benefits go, during my five years as a TM teacher I have come across many people who are deeply grateful to the technique because of what it has done for them and when dealing with these benefits it is to these people I turn, not to the scientific tests. Whenever possible I will let them speak in their own words.

An elderly housewife whom I taught explained the changes this way:

TM to me is rather like being surrounded by a nice soft blanket of security and assurance. I am confident I can handle any kind of situation that arises and remain placid and clear headed. Previous to my becoming involved in TM I slept badly, had bad headaches frequently—nervous indigestion; now—I invariably go to sleep quickly and wake refreshed, I eat well without any disagreeable after effect; I've lots of energy, walk miles with enjoyment, really a new life.

M. C. (Ballinasloe)

While teaching in Dublin I met many people who had had interesting experiences with TM. Such as Mrs R. who, in her personal interview, said a little breathlessly, 'This is not really my choice. My husband has dragged me down here without even asking me if I want to start.'

'And do you want to?'

She nodded. 'When I see what it's done to him in one week, I'll be glad to, only it's *he* who needed it. All our married life he's nearly driven me crazy because he couldn't stay still: every evening, every weekend he was always on the go and insisted that me and the kids go along too—out for a spin, off to the films, the zoo, anywhere as long as he could be on the move. . . and he drove the car like a maniac. I can't tell you how many times I almost left him only he was such a good husband in other ways and I loved him too... then last week he started TM and ever since he's spent his evenings at home quietly. It's unbelievable!'

When she came to the first lecture, her eyes were red rimmed and she came to me quietly afterwards.

'I'm a failure at TM—I haven't stopped crying since I started, not just when I'm doing it but all day long.'

I asked her if she had ever read Longfellow's poem about the Indian brave 'Hiawatha'. She nodded. 'Do you remember when he was killed and his squaw Minehaha sat like one turned to stone? How the old squaws shook their heads over her saying: "If she does not weep, she too will die." Finally when one of them put her baby into her lap it broke the tension and she wept. TM has done the same for you.'

Mrs R. nodded understandingly. 'I didn't know how tense I'd become till this happened. I guess I needed TM as much as he did.'

By the third day Mrs R. was radiant and I couldn't help feeling that their marriage would now start all over again without any bitter recriminations which are so often concomitants of tension still cramping the system even after the stressful situation has gone.

70

Then there was Mr B., a young man of twenty-three, handsome but with a face so dead-looking it was as if carved out of stone. He had been on tranquillisers since the age of seventeen when he had had some nervous trouble. His speech was slow and every time I asked him a question, even though it was simple, it took him a minute to answer: 'Me mates at work make fun of me because I'm so slow,' he said apologetically.

By the third night his face had partially un-frozen. 'When I went into work this morning,' he said, 'me mates said: "Good morning." It's the first time ever. Before, they used to say, "Look who's coming!" But I never told them I was doing TM, so what made them change?'

'Look in a mirror,' I said, 'and you'll see the answer for yourself.'

A few months later I was sitting in a bus and saw him pass by in the street. He was smiling.

There was another youngster I often remember with affection. He was about sixteen, from a poor home and no one else in the family knew or cared about TM. When I asked him what he had got out of it, he replied: 'At my age you change very fast so it's difficult to know what to put down to TM, but two things I'm sure of. One is that I used to be bored to death at weekends without my school-mates round me, but now I like being on my own.

And the other thing I never experienced before was when I saw an aeroplane flying overhead, very high up, glinting silver against the blue and I had a funny feeling here—' he indicated his heart. 'It was beautiful.'

Some benefits are unique, such as the girl who lost her hair through a severe illness and tried for years to grow it again without succees. Some few months after starting TM a thin fluff began to appear on the crown of her head and now she has been able to lay aside the beret she always wore.

Then there was the jockey who explained that if one wanted to get the best out of a horse it was imperative that he should be relaxed. However a horse always picked up his rider's tension and every jockey was tense when he was about to ride in a race.

'I've known many a business man who can *act* relaxed, even when his ulcer's playing him up,' he said wryly, 'and he's fooled many a business rival that way, but by God you can't fool a horse! And that's why I started TM—the change is on the inside, where it really counts!'

Sometimes people are not even aware what they have been missing, until they start the technique, such as the elderly man who discovered to his surprise that he had spent his life in a mild depression and, for the first time ever, began to feel happy in a positive way.

Several people I know who wore glasses have been able to give them up; some who were fat have grown thin and some who were too thin have put on weight though TM teachers will never hold out hopes in any of these directions since it depends on whether the natural tendency of the individual is to be fat or thin.

Sometimes people feel so positively about TM that they are only too pleased to put their approbation into words. Here, for instance, is the verdict of a doctor who has found the TM programme helpful both in his work and in his individual life.

The unique benefits of TM occur, I believe, because it is the most comprehensive system of resting the physiological machine available anywhere. It shows how to handle energy properly or how to recycle energy—our personal energy. So we maximise available energy and become more efficient and better humoured. Ill-health is essentially a lack of energy—a deep-rooted tiredness. We make mistakes when tired. Making mistakes is a simple name for inefficiency—wasting energy and doing very little with the energy we have. . . the most satisfying change to me however, has been gentle, constantly increasing ability to be more aware of everything. The sun (to take a simple example) keeps getting brighter, but also keeps getting more sun-like all the time. It's hard to explain but very satisfying to experience.

I have been particularly impressed by one feature of TM—that the effect has been so gradual and easy. I think this is important because deep fundamental change or growth is gradual.

S. O'C. (Dublin)

Here is the verdict of another doctor just starting out on her career.

I am surrounded by poor communications, low efficiency, unnecessary anxiety; all reflections of stress. As a meditator, expressing the fundamentals of progress, stability, flexibility, growth and integration I am fully aware of the needs and fears of my fellow workers, my patients, my total environment.

TM not only enriches my experience of living but enhances my contribution to society.

S. B. (Cork)

To a business man, subject to long periods under duress and heavy responsibility, TM can be a lifesaver. Here is the opinion of someone who has been practising TM for four years and who owns a chain of large stores:

Verdict. It's the best thing I ever did. It has changed my life. Improvements are excellent in all areas, both home and business, physical and mental.

Physical. When I started TM first I was in a bad state, no energy; even to walk up the stairs was an effort. Quite soon I noticed improvements, and this trend has continued; I've even started to play tennis again.

Business. Calmness under the pressures of daily routine and unexpected happenings is the key to success; TM provides this. In my own experience this calmness grows. In fact one quite enjoys solving problems because the mind is clear.

Home. Good humour and lack of fatigue after a day's work make for better family relationships. So as well as giving oneself to work, one is also able to give oneself to the family. Something which is so often lacking.

E. O'B. (Offaly)

Here is the verdict of an administrator working for a large firm in Northern Ireland:

Business. The feeling of refreshment helps me to tackle the numerous problems occurring on the busy industrial scene in a large company and gives the clarity of thought necessary to understand Government Legislation. . .

Domestic. This was the first area to show improvement and the immediate result was improvement in sleeping habits. The period before the onset of sleep was considerably reduced and the value of sleep improved and made me feel more refreshed. My wife and I became more relaxed at home and this resulted in better marital relations and improved relationship with our four children.

Social. The total quality of life (in a strife-torn country) has improved, there is sharper perception of the natural beauties which surround us, improved tolerance of people and a desire to increase other people's awareness.

D. C. F. (Belfast)

And the final one from the business world was written by a man in a managerial capacity.

. . . What proved stressful situations previous to TM are seldom stressful to me now. Instead of getting uptight under pressure, my mind seems to home in on the kernel of whatever the problem is and the most effective solution of which I am capable of achieving usually emerges. The useless thoughts which buzzed in my mind under stressful situations are gone and a pleasant feeling of calmness is nearly always with me. The capacity to visualise quickly the whole picture in a given situation is increasing and efficiency results.

With TM I find I am more sure of myself in the better sense, am more decisive in making decisions and I have a greater appetite for work. Even on a physical level TM is rewarding. Come home after a busy problem-filled day, tired: do twenty minutes TM and I feel as fresh as if I had gotten a few hours sleep and am ready to enjoy the rest of the evening. Here I would mention another benefit from TM. I no longer carry home in my mind from work the problems of the day—a very nice improvement on pre TM days.

J. W. (Edenderry)

And here is a letter from a woman who has started her own successful business since taking up the TM technique:

TM helped to cure my fifteen-year-old ulcers. Improved my general disposition, relations with people and makes me feel good. In my work situation, working in a textile production with its usual pressures, etc; through TM I can find that still point which enables me to solve problems, see to the needs of my employees and enjoy creativity on the job.

J. T. (Wicklow)

A lecturer in social studies in a Dublin University has this to say:

As a professional social worker I have naturally been interested in self-development. Social work is concerned with helping people achieve their potential but I am not aware of any social work technique which can compare to TM. It is the most effective technique for self-actualisation of which I am aware. It also has the distinct advantage of scientific validation of its effectiveness.

For me TM is like a key that has unlocked what is inside me and my life has been filled with increasing happiness and fulfilment in the three years since I started the practice. I have felt the many doubts, fears and anxieties which haunted me gradually dissolve. I have felt myself become a fuller person—more open to others and more appreciative of them, more positive in my feelings towards myself, more confident, better humoured. The confusion has given way to quietness that underlies everything. I am able to perceive things more quickly and clearly. I feel that I am using more of my intelligence. I have more energy and enthusiasm.

R. C. (Dublin)

The final verdict on the benefits should, I feel, go to the people who are most aware of the golden thread inherent in the TM programme. First, the clergyman: Fr O'R. started to meditate six years ago and has this to say:

... as a religious, it changed my prayer life considerably to a deeper quieter type of prayer that I never dreamt possible for me. I learned the art of being content to be in the presence of God in a restful attentive silence. I know now that there are many Christian prayer traditions that could have taught me this way of prayer, but I never thought that they were for an ordinary fellow like me. I see TM as a very simple technique that facilitates a natural spontaneous tendency in all human beings towards greater and greater happiness and therefore as not tied to any religious belief. But being a Christian myself, I use it as an instrument to make me a better Christian.

Overall, TM has given me: (1) an increased interest in mystical traditions, particularly Christian; (2) a deeper centering of myself, you might say a sort of unflappability; and (3) a heightened awareness of the possibilty of deeper prayer for myself and for the everyday Christian.

78

Sr P. O'S. (Co. Meath) confirms this impression of the deepening of religious feeling:

I started to practise TM two and a half years ago and have found tremendous inner peace and tranquility. Having had two serious illnesses I was very conscious of the healing effect of TM on the body and the mind. I, as a religious, have found that my committment means much more to me. People, environment and living are vital. Boundaries of differences and intolerances have diminished. In fact the 'I have come that you may have life and have it more abundantly' seems to be the most natural thing in the world.

And finally the comments of two ordinary people who also found the 'golden thread'. First, the widow with three children, who was one of my first pupils:

I find that TM has changed my whole life. I find I am much closer to God. I can accept his will much easier. . .

The musician, from whom I quoted earlier, also mentions this aspect,

TM helped me to find a purpose in life—to live my life to the full; to be happy deep within myself, without constantly seeking another person who would make me happy. It has brought me closer to God, not just having to go to a church to find him, but to realise that 'the Kingdom of God is (really) within' and we can find God everywhere, all around us any time.

As for myself, brought up without a religion and haunted by the questions: Who am I? and Who made the solar system?, what effect has TM had on solving these imponderables? At least now I know fully who I am, and though I would still categorise myself as an agnostic, I see the absurdity of fitting people and ideas into categories since the stillness I have experienced at the deepest level of myself is the same that exists in the centre of everyone else. I am also aware, as a creative artist, that this still centre is the source of all my acts of creation. The seemingly impossible statement that out of nothing can come something is no longer a contradiction— I *know* it to be true. Also wherever I look in nature I see this same pattern of creativity taking place: plants appearing, growing to fullness and falling back into nothingness. Thus I feel a growing conviction, not intellectually but on a level of the heart, that every part of the universe is governed by the same principle—emerging, becoming and falling back into stillness. And since I have experienced the fulfilling of nature of this stillness and know that it is indestructible (as it is no thing then nothing can destroy it) and since it is my Self, what is death but a return to Self and what is there to fear in life, since my Self is indestructible?

6 The Sidhis

It is of course one thing to experience briefly in activity the transcendental peace that lies within, and quite another to operate from that transcendental level throughout the twenty-four hours of the day which is the avowed aim of those in the TM Movement who are following the golden thread. This level of consciousness is referred to as Cosmic Consciousness and it presupposes that you have released all the stress that was in your system. Already there are many thousands of people who have achieved this goal.

It is quite impossible to analyse how far along the road one has come because one never knows how much stress is waiting to be released. The best that can be done is to follow the rules and hope for the best. During my eight years of TM I noticed that my mind had quietened down, even in the most agitated activity, and the ageing process also seemed to have slowed down; indeed the lines on my face have become less, not more.

But one area of stress that did not alter was the osteo-arthritis that thrust an occasional knife into my shoulder blades, was causing small nodules to grow on my finger joints and making it ever more difficult to turn my head, apart from the crunching of the crystals between the vertebrae when I did so. Sometimes I wondered if I had started TM too late to cure myself of this stress-symbol.

But help was in sight. During the short period of my teaching in Dublin I heard of some new courses being held at the Maharishi European Research Unit (M.E.R.U) in Seelisberg, Switzerland. They were called Governor Training Courses and lasted six months. No one knew quite what was going on but there was plenty of conjecture and the vibrations were so electric that the moment I heard about them, I felt that restless inner urge being activated. The impulse was so strong that not even the fact that I would be six months away from home at a cost of over £2000 could discourage me. Gradually all impediments dissolved and in October 1976 I entered the Maharishi European Research Unit (M.E.R.U.)

In my six months there, startling changes took place. As well as getting rid of most of my arthritis, I was beginning to experience the 'silent state' even in activity.

How did these changes come about? By means

of a new and powerful technique called the *Sidhis*.

The reason for the introduction of the *Sidhis* was thus: The TM Movement was now eighteen years old and as a result of the deep rest gained during the practice, a lot of stress had been released by a lot of people, particularly teachers who had attended many intensive meditation courses as part of their teaching programme. Maharishi felt that the time had now come to expand the benefits with a more powerful technique and for the previous two years he had been experimenting with some thousands of teachers on the best means of introducing it.

The new programme had been well researched and documented. M.E.R.U. owned some of the most sophisticated apparatus in the world for measuring and computing the physiological changes that took place inside people as they practised both TM and the *Sidhis*. There was also a team of scientists and doctors working with Maharishi, attracted by this exciting new field of research: the physiology of enlightenment.

The originator of the *Sidhis* technique was a sage of the second century B.C. called Patanjali, who wrote one of the most famous classics in Vedic literature, the *Great Commentary*. He was also thought to be the originator of the exercises practised all over the world under the name of *Yoga*.

The difference between TM and the *Sidhis* lies in this: in TM the mind moves automatically to a state of deep quietness and in the *Sidhis* technique, this quietness is activated. As we know from science, the energy stored in an object at the refined atomic level is much greater than that contained in the grosser aspects. For instance, you can burn a bucket of coal in a grate in a very short time without releasing much heat and yet this same quantity of coal, if converted at the most refined level would yield twenty-five billion kilowatt hours of electricity or as much power as all the power plants in the US could generate in two months.

In the same way, if we activate our minds on a refined level the more powerful our thought become.

Sidhis is a Sanscrit word meaning 'abilities' and the abilities referred to are those usually termed supernormal, such as precognition, bilocation, intuition, levitation and feelings of unity with all living things. Maharishi insists that these are the abilities of a normal man, a man who is free from stress. Those who have stress in their systems—such as my arthritic condition—are deemed the subnormal ones.

Most of the Course Participants were young, healthy and had done more rounding courses than I had; even so we were not judged ready to receive the new technique until the course was half over. The effect was explosive: some, while sitting in the lotus position (with the legs tied into a sort of knot) began to lift off the ground. Some were flooded with light and some had feelings of being overwhelmed with love. For me the effect was different: I shook from head to foot, but mostly head and shoulders, sometimes with such severity that I felt like a rag-doll in the hands of a child suffering from tantrums. As the weeks went by the crunching noise in my neck, as I rolled my head, became less and less and the nodules on my fingers began to shrink. This experience convinced me that if the body can be put naturally into a deep enough state of rest, it knows how to heal itself. I was not the only one whose arthritis made spectacular improvements; a young American girl whose arthritic condition had been well documented on X-rays was also cured and indeed the whole course was amazed at the rapid healing taking place in many different categories.

One of the differences between TM and the *Sidhis* is that whereas we practise TM on our own, the *Sidhis* is a group activity. The reason is that on this refined level thoughts are very powerful and whatever level is gained by the most evolved member of the group draws the others like a magnet: in much the same way can a captain inspire his team to perform at their optimum level. Infinite correlation is the term given to this phenomenon and when my bouts of shaking became less, I too felt this correlation raising me to higher levels, even on a physical plane. During the practice I sometimes felt the following sequence of experiences: all activity in my body would cease and physical boundaries appeared to vanish. I would feel myself melting into such a flow of softness and love it was like a distillation of happiness. It was at that point I felt a force lifting me momentarily off the ground.

Sometimes these experiences would come in activity, such as when I saw a squirrel running up a tree and I *was* the squirrel feeling the rough bark under my nails. As the practice continued I felt this unity with all living things often recurring.

The six month's course concluded with a conference when we were told that the *Sidhis* technique was going to be made available, not simply for teachers, but for anyone who had been meditating at least six months. A pre-requisite for learning was that they had completed eight specially structured weeklong courses, so upon returning home I set up a series of such courses in our Arts Centre. The structure was powerful and the results, striking: some who attended began to experiences feelings of love and happiness that were new to them.

I feel a great flowing of love for everyone, even for people that I never got on with too well before.

D. M. (Dublin)

Some began to experience life on a very refined level.

My vision of things around me and my feelings for everything is changing quite dramatically. Sometimes I have felt as though all life around me was just pure light. . . sometimes blue light, and I would feel as if I were just a ray or a wave of light myself. The cumulative effect of these experiences has given me a deeper understanding of myself. Sometimes I have experienced a burning intense love for God or for whoever Being really is.

M. C. (Dublin)

These are not people who have been meditating a long time, nor had they done any long rounding programmes. They come from all walks of life and sometimes with heavy family commitments, such as P. G. from Limerick who is a married woman with a baby of a few months and a child under two years. Her husband is a farmer and this year they are letting out their lands for grazing so that they can take it in turns to look after the children and attend the requisite number of preparatory *Sidhis* weeks, of which there are many now running in Ireland. When I asked P. G. why they had taken such a decisive measure, she replied: 'We want the children to feel the benefit of our increasing harmony while they are still small.'

I knew she was right, remembering with dismay how angry I used to get with mine when they were small, although I knew intrinsically that the effect of my rage was destructive. Psychologists say that a child's whole life is conditioned by what happens in its first two years. A loving start in childhood makes for a harmonious life, a battered beginning predisposes towards violence and disharmony. On the last course P. G. had many beautiful experiences: here is one.

As I started to meditate, I had a few of the usual thoughts—then I felt a sudden gush of light entering my being—I felt I had transcended and was held captive in this area of great charm— every bit of me was alert to this state—enveloped in a radiant amber blanket of pure Bliss. I stayed almost without a breath enjoying the immensity, the fullness, the purity and radiant love. It has become increasingly difficult to come out of meditations—so captivating is the charm in them. I feel infinitely blessed.

7   Everyone needs TM

Sometimes in Introductory Talks people say: 'What could TM do for me? I'm young, happy, healthy, relatively free of stress, have good relationships with my family and friends and am successful at my job. What more could I want?'

TM teachers always reply that scientists claim we are only using ten to fifteen per cent of our potential and TM opens up the other eighty-five per cent. This I feel is a very dry answer so when I came upon three letters written by a young solicitor who filled all the above categories of not needing TM and found what he had gained by learning the technique, I thought it useful to include it as a postscript for all healthy, happy, successful individuals who are wondering what it would do for them.

The letters were written at irregular intervals, without any thought of publication. Between letters one and two the writer had taken four weeks of the preparatory *Sidhis* courses. Between two and three there was a gap of four months which indicates that gains achieved at the course are now a permanent feature of his life.

Letter one:

... Transcendental meditation—what a different meaning that word conjures up now, four years after I started to meditate.

The first time I ever heard the word was in America and like so many others, its first connection was with the Beatles. The connection intrigued me, not like so many others because of its sensational and newsy aspect but rather why India? Why the new interest in the East? What did the East offer that Western Civilisation, religion and philosophy lacked?

Well the answer took a little while to develop and it wasn't until after I meditated that it became clear: it was that no matter how much one might try, peace and contentment come not from an outward journey but rather an inward one, the route to peace and happiness lies so obviously within oneself. When one is one's own best friend everything is in harmony.

The above is a general background as to how I became involved. In the beginning, being honest, it was difficult. I was still studying and doing exams and I always felt I didn't have enough time. This process went on for a year and a half until I eventually decided that I would either do it properly or give it up altogether.

In retrospect, without a shadow of doubt the best thing I ever did. Its immediate effect was a very superficial although important one. It gave me order, something I had always aspired to but could never put into proper operation. (TM)... gave me two periods of mental activity (during which I was neither awake in the sense of being involved in the outside world, nor asleep, in the sense of not being involved in a cognitive aspect) when all the confusion and cloudiness of the day would just melt away and at the end of it, leave one's mind clear and rested. I later formed my own analogy about this—to me, the two periods were like two bridges between the land of confusion and frustration and the land of harmony. It was such an easy thing to pass over and rest one's mind.

It is important to note that it's usually some time before one actually 'knows' a change in oneself but external aspects become great indicators. The appearance of one's face, the recognition of the stupidity of so many needless arguments, the insignificance of so many so called important things in life—

In the internal sense, the growing knowledge of what is good and bad for one, be it food or rest or whatever. The wonderful enjoyment of whatever activity one might be involved in, the knowledge that it is only because of tiredness or frustration that one can't enjoy every minute of every day.

Applying it to my work I could only count on one hand the number of times in the past two years that I felt I didn't actually want to go to work. One would arrive in the morning with an enthusiastic attitude to the task at hand and if one didn't succeed one never felt demoralised but rather more interested in finding out why one hadn't succeeded as one's mind became less and less concerned about unrealities.

One began to quickly realise when one was doing too much but one always knew that this would just be washed away in one's evening meditation, when one would literally forget and be unconcerned with one's daily activities be they of yesterday or tomorrow, if to think of same was a useless rather than constructive activity. . .

I could go on ad infinitum; suffice it to say that it gives to each person the opportunity to unveil and apply their full talents, in the knowledge that the use of the same is not to measure one's success against another's but to fulfill oneself.

Letter two.

. . . I have changed; of that there is no doubt but to use such a word as change devalues what has happened; discovered and realised and bathed in certain pools of myself would be better. I am astounded at what I have found. There was no doubt that during the last week of the course I began to feel and experience things very deeply within myself and for the first time since I left Schull, I have found it difficult to verbalise it to others; I know it and it knows me and anyone who knows it within themselves also knows it is in me and I in them. . . I thought it so precious when I left that I visualised it as a glass box and hoped that it would not fall and break. I always wondered how diluted it would become as the days went by and was excited to see how it stood up in outside activity. Well, if anything the glass box has become unbreakable. . . and the ignorance of my intellect is gradually giving way to the growing enlightenment of my intellect. . . (I shall) be thankful for the rest of my life just to have had a glimpse of what manner life should be and how wonderful it is to live in love and harmony. . .

Letter three.
. . . Life could not be more wonderful and fulfilling. Each day is full to the brim with laughter of the heart, the eyes and the soul and the aura of peace and tranquility one carries with one after meditation is growing daily.

T.M. (Dublin)

93

References

CHAPTER TWO

1. Pierre Teilhard de Chardin, *On Happiness*, London: Collins, 1973.

2. Henri Troyat, *Tolstoy*, Pelican Biographies, 1970.

SELECTED LIST OF BOOKS
FOR FURTHER READING

Maharishi Mahesh Yogi, *The Science of Being and Art of Living*, SRM Publications, 1963.

Maharishi Mahesh Yogi, *On the Bhagavad Gita*, A New Translation and Commentary. Chapters 1-6. Penguin, 1967.

Peter Russell, *The TM Technique*, Routledge and Kegan Paul, 1976.

Jack Forem, *Transcendental Meditation*, George Allen and Unwin Ltd, 1974.

Anthony Campbell, *Seven States of Consciousness*, Gollancz, 1973.

Anthony Campbell, *The Mechanics of Enlightenment*, Gollancz, 1975.

Bloomfield & Cain, *TM Discovering Inner Energy and Overcoming Stress*, Delacorte Press, New York, 1975.

Bloomfield & Kory, *Happiness: TM Program. Psychiatry and Enlightenment*, Dawn Press, Simon & Schuster, New York, 1976.

Denniston & McWilliams, *The TM Book: How to Enjoy the Rest of Your Life*, Versemonger Press, 1975.

Robbins & Fisher, *Tranquility Without Pills*, Peter Wyden, 1972.

Una Kroll, *TM: A Signpost for the World*, Darton, Longman & Todd, 1974.

NATIONAL TM CENTRES

For particulars of your nearest centre write to the National Office:

Ireland:
   MIU (Ireland) Ltd, 10 Trafalgar Terrace, Monkstown, Co. Dublin. Telephone: (01) 808333.

Northern Ireland:
   TM Centre, 120 Malone Avenue, Belfast BT8 6ET Telephone: (084) 660953.

England:
   Maharishi International College, Roydon Hall, East Peckham, Tonbridge, Kent TN12 5NH. Telephone: (0622) 813243 or 813073.

THE PURSUIT OF MEANING
Joseph Fabry

The Pursuit of Meaning is written for the millions of people who are healthy but believe they are sick, because they feel empty; for those who are looking for meaning in frantic activity, in money, power, speed, excitement, sex, alcohol, and drugs, or in the pursuit of happiness for happiness' sake; for those who are looking for meaning in laws and rules and dogmas rather than searching for it personally. Every mature person has been expelled from his own paradise and lived through his own concentration camp. To help man endure this has always been the task of prophets, priests, philosophers and educators. Now they are joined by psychologists. Logotherapy supplies one contemporary answer to man's age-old problem of how to live after the expulsion and how to find meaning during and after the trials of sufferings.

The Pursuit of Meaning is a guide to the theory and application of Viktor E. Frankl's logotherapy and is a very readable book which will appeal to anyone interested in the purpose of life. It is an excellently and clearly written, authoritative and comprehensive presentation of Frankl's system, probably more complete than can be found in any one volume by Frankl himself. It was first published in English in the USA and is now in its third edition. It has been translated and published in Italian, German, Spanish and Japanese.

ENJOY A HAPPY MARRIAGE
Tony Baggot, S.J.

From *Enjoy a Happy Marriage* you can learn about :

— the making of a marriage ....
— the meaning of personal intimacy ......
— accepting feelings ....
— the effect of other feelings on sex........
— The strength and weakness of man and woman ....
— the place of forgiveness ....
— the influence of past experiences on the present ....
— our changing style of marriage ....

Those about to marry and those already married will find guidance in this book for sorting out their thoughts and feelings. As partners do this they will become closer to each other and so will enjoy a happy marriage.

Now as always people wish to marry but are less ready than before to endure an unsatisfactory situation. They set out to enjoy marriage but often without being clear about what they want or how to go about it.

THE GOD I DON'T BELIEVE IN
Juan Arias

The modern world, it is clear, has gradually developed a completely different approach to God and the Supernatural. We no longer think of Divine Providence riding the clouds in the distant heavens, but as a Father understandable in human terms: warm, accessible, non-authoritarian — a God for all men who have grown weary of the ancient image of an implacable Jehovah.

This 'new' and 'credible' God is the subject of this book — a book which will make, in its warmth and feeling, immediate contact with the reader.

'A real joy; something superb. One must only read it; and then let his heart speak' — *Fruili* (Italian).

Already in Italian, French, German, Portuguese — and now in English, *The God I Don't Believe in* is addressed — with gusto — to all contemporary Christians.

PRAYER WITHOUT FRILLS
Juan Arias

Prayer Without Frills is meant to be a cry of rage and a cry of joy — at one and the same time.

It is *prayer* because it expresses, in words, man's deepest needs and feelings.

It is *without frills* because it does not follow any set patterns, conventions or cultural or religious prejudices. It is simply the real words of every human being who, face to face with the reality of his existence, cries out without fear, without shame and with all the power of his inalienable freedom, everything that he feels is in contradiction to what others impose on him.

It is the prayer of the man who discovers that praying does not mean that he consents to being enslaved *by* anyone or *for* any reason.

It is the prayer of the man who discovers that his God has given him the right to pray, not to beg as an alms but to demand that happiness which God, in a mystery of love, promised him freely, asking only that he accept it.

These prayers spring from the experiences of actual men and women; and they express what many other people are saying as they walk the roads of life, crying aloud to their God and their conscience, searching for solace and newness.